DISCOVERING THE ROAD TO YOUR DESTINY

FROM PAIN, TO PURPOSE, TO PROMISE

BY SANDRA F. MOORE

Kingdom Journey Press
A Division of Kingdom Journey Enterprises
Woodbridge, VA

Unless a person is explicitly identified by name, the statements that are used should not be directly attributed to any specific person.

Unless otherwise marked, all scripture quotations are referenced from the King James Version of the Bible.

ISBN-10: 0982700180
ISBN-13: 978-0-9827001-8-1

Printed in the United States of America.
Published by Kingdom Journey Press
A Division of Kingdom Journey Enterprises, Woodbridge, VA
www.kjpressinc.com

Cover Design by Brand U Inc.
www.branduinc.com

Dedication

I dedicate this book to the
memory of my dad, Walter Hill Jr.

Not only was I the first born child,
I was blessed to be born on his birthday.

Dad you were a great encourager to me. The last
words you spoke to me were "Where is your faith"?
All I can say, is God is strengthening my faith daily.
Your words will always remain in my heart,
and I will never forget them as long as I live!

For I know the plans I have for you,
declares the Lord,
plans for welfare and not for evil,
to give you a future and a hope.
(Jeremiah 29:11, ESV)

Table of Contents

Foreword

Wendy and I are honored to write the foreword for such a visionary and awesome woman of God. Sandra Moore has not begun to scratch the surface on the potential God has placed in her in sharing her heart and ministry with the world. She has a sincere desire to reach the masses through her writings. It's at this time, in this economy, in this hour that we, as a people, need to search within ourselves to find out who we really are and what makes us tick. We have had the opportunity to read *Discovering the Road to Your Destiny,* and we are convinced that this book will change the life of any reader who picks it up and begin to internalize the meaning and words on each page. This read is timely and certain to alter the course of millions of people. The average individual either does not know or has not discovered his/her destiny. In other words, they don't know why they were created. Each of us has been called to a specific undertaking in this life. Yes, God has personally chosen each of us to assume a role and perform it to perfection. Some examples are worth sharing to bring home the point;

selected individuals have the gift of singing, acting, dancing, teaching, preaching, leading, directing, or managing. What is your calling? More importantly, what is your destiny? In what direction are your headed? As you turn the pages in this text, allow the Holy Scriptures referenced and the encouragement given to replace your inflexible demeanor and perspective on life. The scriptures remind us that we are more than conquerors in Christ Jesus. So, read, relax, and replace old ideas with new ones as they help you discover who you really are in Christ Jesus. To our spiritual daughter, Sandra: You are a timely jewel in God's hand. It's your time! It's your season! Walk in your destiny.

Barry & Wendy Mitchell
Spiritual Parents

Reviews & Endorsements

Many times in life we are faced with the unexpected and the unacceptable. There are challenges, ups and downs, direct and indirect attacks. There is always a positive or negative approach when dealing with life. Sandra has used the gift that God has given her to bring the reader to a positive approach, victorious mindset and a decision making process based on the Word of God. There is no way that you can read this book and not see the light at the end of your tunnel. I thank God that Sandra allowed Him to pour into her so that she could pour into the pages of this much needed book. It is no coincidence that God has blessed us with her and this book during this time in history. We are all in need of edification, exhortation and comfort. Sandra, may God continue to bless you as you allow yourself to be available for Him.

~Pastor Judith M. Kithcart
Overseer-Pure N' Heart Ministries

Every person needs to read this spirit-filled message that God has given my dear friend Sandra F. Moore. I believe that most of us have experienced some challenging times in life that had us question our very existence. This book is a blessing as it reveals that even out of pain there is purpose for us that is far greater than what we can see with the natural eye. Get ready for your life to be transformed after reading this book!

~Minister Shontel. D. Wood

Sandra Moore's first novel, *Discovering the Road To Your Destiny,* is a roadmap for anyone who wants to understand their purpose in life and discover their God-given destiny. Ms. Moore gives us candid insight into the pain that life brings God's purpose for our lives and His divine promises to us. Born out of personal pain and triumphs, this book is a must-read for everyone that seeks healing and deliverance.

~Kim M. Johnson, MD, Associate Director,
Healing Rooms of Woodbridge, Woodbridge, VA

Discovering the Road To Your Destiny is truly an eye opener and a book that will encourage many along the way. I believe this book is one that others will read and say, "Wow, I thought I was the only one who encountered these obstacles, but now I know that I'm not." I thank God for Sandra's transparency about real life encounters that will cause readers to be encouraged to know that they too can make it. By reading this book, they will know that their experiences are just a process that we must go through in order to fulfill the destiny and plans God has for us.

~Minister Sonia Mayo

I have known Sister Sandra Moore for a long time. I have seen and walked with her through life's ups and downs. She has endured heartaches, joy and pain, yet she always prevailed with the help of God. The three characters throughout this book explain not only what Sister Sandra Moore has experienced, but what we all must go through in life. The battle of the mind is what we all toil with in decision making. The heart brings about love and pain, once the decisions are made. (Weeping may endure for the night but joy comes in the morning.) Last but the most important is the courage to lean not to your own understanding, and trust in the Lord and the power of His might. What a great woman behind a great book.

~ Elder Jennifer Merritt

Acknowledgements

First and foremost, I thank God who is the author and finisher of my life, the Alpha and Omega, my everything, the one and only living God; who has never left me nor forsaken me. Thank you Lord!

To my loving mother and best friend, Sarah Hill, without you, there would be no me. I thank God for your love and faithfulness in all the little things you do. Thank you for always being by my side and for instilling in me much love, wisdom and knowledge. Love you unconditionally!!!

To my late grandmother Ethel Harris (The Intercessor), who led me to Christ at a young age, and who was ***always*** praying. Thank you for your unconditional love, wisdom and your prayers.

To my lovely children Carolyn, Tony, Nigel and Lionel Jr., who are my inspiration and the pride & joy of my life. My little angels my grandchildren, Keyonni, Keyon, Juliette, Tatyana, Kajayah, Kaziah, and Kavonna. I love you *ALL* unconditionally!!! Thank you Lord for the 11 disciples you have blessed me with!

To my siblings, Gloria, Antoinette, Walter and Dale. My Aunt Edna Bozeman, Uncle James Harris, and Pastor T.J. Hill, and a host of nieces, nephews and cousins. I thank God for the opportunity to minister in your lives. Be encouraged and keep the faith. Much love to you all!

To my spiritual parents and mentors Deacon Barry and Pastor Wendy Mitchell. I thank God for appointing you as my spiritual parents. Thank you for pushing and stretching me to where God is taking me and for being there for me in so many ways. Love you!

To the Wailing Women and Men Ministry, which has been a blessing from the Lord. I appreciate each and every one of you, and cannot express how I have been truly blessed by this ministry.

To my spiritual sisters MWOG (Sonia, Kim, Shontel). I thank God for putting some of the most anointed and powerful praying women in my life. Thank you all for the kindness that you have shown, for being there to support me and for always being there when I needed someone to pray with and talk to.

To my prophet mentor, Prophet James Kithcart, who always reminded me who I am in Christ, no matter what people may say. Thank you Sir for the many words of encouragement. Your encouragement has validated my dreams. God bless you and your family!

There are so many others who have been a blessing in my life that I have not mentioned. By all means know that I have not forgotten you. I thank God for each of you, and appreciate you!

I thank God for this awesome Woman of God, Casandra Johnson, Founder and CEO of Kingdom Journey Press Publishing Company, for helping to make this vision plain. This is the beginning of my God given Destiny! Thank you and May God continuously bless you and your ministries!

Introduction

Life is a journey filled with lessons, hardships, heartaches, joys, celebrations and special moments that will ultimately lead us to our destination and purpose in life. The road will not always be smooth; in fact, throughout our journey, we will encounter many challenges. These challenges will test our courage, strengths, weaknesses, and faith.

On this journey we will be confronted with many situations. Some will be filled with joy, and some will be filled with heartaches, however the way we react to what we are faced with determines what kind of outcome the rest of our journey through life will be like.

When things don't go our way, we have two choices. We can focus on the fact that things didn't go how we expected and then allow life to pass us by, or we can make the best of the situation and know that God is there to see us through. These are only temporary setbacks, in hope that we find the lessons that are to be learned.

When I think of this journey that we have to accomplish, I think about the Wizard of Oz. Many of us can relate to the story and know that Dorothy's journey was not easy. Neither is our Christian walk. It brings us to the absolute end of ourselves and to the place of doing the perfect will which God has called us to do. One thing we must remember is it's not about us at all, but it's all about giving God glory and honoring Him because of who He is.

Know that if we remain focused, the trials and tribulations we face will not stop us from fulfilling what God has purposed for our lives.

It's because of the heartaches, as well as the hardships, that will help make us stronger and lead us further into our God given destiny.

> *Beloved, do not think it strange concerning the fiery trial which is to try you, as though some strange thing happened to you; but rejoice to the extent that you partake of Christ's sufferings, that when His glory is revealed, you may also be glad with exceeding joy. (1 Peter 4:12-13)*

Let's look at the three characters Dorothy encountered on her journey. The first one she met was the Scarecrow. In meeting him, he told her that he didn't have a brain; at least he thought he didn't.

When we give our lives to Christ, we become born again Christians, meaning, that we can no longer operate with the worldly mind we once had. Just like the scarecrow who thought he didn't have a brain, we as Christians can no longer have the mindset of the world. Our mind must be completely transformed to the mind of Christ, and the only way to replace our way of thinking like the world is to replace it with God's truth, and the only infallible source of God's truth is found in His Word.

And be not conformed to this world: but be ye transformed by the renewing of your mind, that ye may prove what is that good, and acceptable, and perfect, will of God. (Romans 12:2)

Renewing your mind from all the worldly garbage is important so you can clearly hear the voice of God when He speaks to you and commands you to do what He has purposed for your life so that you can move into your God given destiny.

Part of renewing our minds is learning who we are in Christ, gaining wisdom, knowledge, and understanding, especially the knowledge of His will. That is why it is so important that we renew our minds by meditating on God's Word daily.

The second character was the Tin Man, who didn't have a heart. Just like our minds had to be transformed, our hearts have to be restored and cleaned up.

Prior to giving our life to Christ, many of us were heartless. What I mean by heartless is we may have had bitterness, or unforgiveness, or been unkind, spiritless and disheartened. In so many ways we were like the tin man who didn't have a caring heart, but we too thought we had it all together.

Your heart includes your mind, will, and emotions. The enemy wants you to become distrusting, offended, disillusioned, and hurt, so that you will harden your heart to God and to others. Hardness of heart separates us from love and relationships, and makes us bitter and jealous. A clean, pure heart is essential to serving God, and to having a right relationship with God.

> *Blessed are the pure in heart, for they will see God. (Matthew 5:8)*

In order for us to have a pure heart, God has to perform surgery on our heart to cleanse us from all indwelling sin. We must first repent of all our sins, forgive those who have hurt us, and begin living a life that is pleasing to God. This cannot be done in our own strength.

Pray and ask God to create in you a clean heart and renew a steadfast spirit within you. Ask for total forgiveness; that's forgiving others as well as yourself, and to strengthen you in the areas where you are weak. Let Him perform complete surgery on your heart.

> *Create in me a clean heart, O God; and renew a right spirit within me.(Psalm 51:10)*

Your heart is what creates that beautiful character inside you. You will start to become more of a passionate person. You will demonstrate love for people that you thought you never had.

Forgiving people will become so much easier. The most important thing you will see is an increase in your relationship with God. He wants to be involved in all areas of your life. Open your heart and let the presence of God shine!

Lastly, was the Cowardly Lion. He didn't have courage. To sum it up, he was fearful.

But He said to them, "Why are you fearful, O' you of little faith?" (Matthew 8:26)

Many times in our walk with Christ, we don't have the courage or the faith to step out into the things God has called us to do because of fear. Joshua 1:9 says:

Have I not commanded you? Be strong and courageous. Do not be frightened, and do not be dismayed, for the Lord your God is with you wherever you go.

With this said, what is our problem??? God's Word stated clearly that He has not given us a spirit of fear, but of power and of love and of a sound mind.

It is only in our walking out on faith that the path of God will open ahead of us. In this book you will understand that in your pain there is a purpose, and once you begin to fulfill God's purpose for your life, you will see the manifestation of His promises in your life like never before.

So wherever you are now in your life, if you are at a cross road regarding any decisions that you have to take, pray about it, seek His face, and heed to the voice of God for direction. Step out on faith, do not fear, but trust the leading of our God and know that you are on the road to your destiny!!!

Chapter 1. The Pain

> *Woe is me for my hurt! My wound is grievous and incurable: But I say, truly this is a grief, and I must bear it. (Jeremiah 10:19)*

No one is exempt from pain. It does not matter whether it is pain from sickness, pain from the loss of a loved one, pain from losing a job, pain from rejection, pain from going through a divorce or pain from our own sins. No matter the form of pain, it is still pain!

Did you know that harboring pain can cause a lot of disappointments and sickness in life? We often hear the term "Let go and let God", but how does someone do that? I will explain this in a later chapter.

We have to be aware of our emotions and feelings while in pain. Pain can produce shame, guilt, fear, anger and negative thoughts which can lead to depression and other illnesses. Feelings of hurt and pain can cause you to do or say things that you may later regret. You have to truly learn how to let go and let God be in control of your situation. Turn your pain over to Him. He will never put more on you than what He knows you are able to bear.

> *No temptation has overtaken you except such as is common to man; but God is faithful, who will not allow you to be tempted beyond what you are able, but with the temptation will also make the way of*

escape, that you may be able to bear it. (1 Corinthians 10:13, NKJV)

We may not understand the trials and tribulations we are going through, but we need to understand the source of our suffering before we can experience the blessings that God has for us in the midst of our pain. To prevent the pain from controlling our emotions and lives, we must learn to speak the Word of God over our situations, and trust and believe that God will do just what He says He will do. We hear about grace, trust and belief, however we have to learn how to work the principles in order to get the results of the plan that God has for our lives.

And God is able to make all grace abound to you, so that in all things at all times, having all that you need, you will abound in every good work. (2 Corinthians 9:8)

PAIN DURING SICKNESS

Pain is often a symptom of an illness. A specific condition such as chronic back pain or coughing and chest congestion that are typically associated with having a common cold is the physical suffering a person experiences as a result of the sickness. Sickness is something every one may experience at one time or another during their life. There are many sicknesses that may cause your body to experience great pain. Many of us can not deal with pain, not even the simplest pain, without murmuring and complaining.

When someone asks you how you are feeling, the first thing that a person who is not feeling well might say is "I'm not feeling well", "My back hurts", or "I have a cold". STOP IT!!! Proverbs 18:21 tells us:

Death and life are in the power of the tongue:
and they that love it shall eat the fruit thereof.

I am not saying that we have to be in denial that we are sick, but we must use our words wisely. Remember, the words we speak are very powerful, so why speak sickness over your life instead of believing God to His Word. By His stripes we are healed. It is already done.

Last year, I was diagnosed with high blood pressure. I could have responded negatively by saying such things as, "Oh, I have high blood pressure," or "Oh well, it runs in the family". By doing so, I would have been accepting the doctor's report. Instead, I made a decision that I was going to stand on what I believe, and believe the report of the Lord that I am healed. The doctor had a strange look as she reviewed my chart. Then she repeated it again, but I still did not receive it. She asked why I would say I did not have high blood pressure, when it was clearly stated in my chart that I did. I told her that the Word of God says that I am healed by His stripes. At that time she began to laugh and stated that she agreed. After going back a week later for a follow up, my blood pressure had returned back to normal. Glory be to God!

Note that, the high blood pressure did not just go away over night. There were some things I needed to accomplish in order to overcome the sickness.

Praying and asking for God's healing in any situation should always be your first resort. I began to pray and believe God for His divine intervention and healing.

Then I had to change my lifestyle by eating healthy and exercising regularly. These key points played a major role in lowering my blood pressure. As we know, we cannot do it in our own strength. God has also given mankind wisdom to treat all manner of sickness and disease. Always trust and believe that you are healed in the process by faith.

We must have faith in God through it all, even when things may not seem to be changing. In Matthew 11:28, Jesus was very specific in telling those who were heavy-laden and overburdened to come to Him. If we are experiencing fear and doubt, it's because we are not trusting God. How can we trust Him in some things and not in others? God is sovereign ALL the time, not some of the time.

When we need a miracle in our situation, then we must realize that God is the only one that can perform that miracle. We must go to Him in prayer, casting all our cares on Him, and trust that He will handle it all, in His way, and in His timing, which is always on time. We must stop harboring over the situation and start trusting.

> *Now faith is confidence in what we hope for and assurance about what we do not see. (Hebrews 11:1)*

God wants us to trust and believe Him to fulfill His plan during the most difficult time in our life. It won't be easy though, therefore we must fight in faith to stand on God's Word that we are healed. Paul said that we must, "Fight the good fight of faith" (1 Tim. 6:12). Faith can move mountains!

We know how the doctors like to refer to our family's history to determine why we have certain aliments or diseases. Well, they don't look back far enough. If they did, they would know that we as Christians have the DNA (the blood) of our Spiritual Father which has all the power to overcome all sicknesses and diseases.

> *And the LORD will take away from thee all sickness. (Deuteronomy 7:15)*

If He says it is His will, will He not do it? All we need to do is stand on the Word of God, trust and believe that He is our source and know that by the power of His Word that by Jesus' stripes, we are healed. Once we know this, then nothing in life will be too hard for us. AMEN!!!

PAIN FROM DIVORCE

Divorce is a very painful experience. It creates our deepest fears of being abandoned, rejected and unloved, and it destroys years of invested love and care for that person. It also causes anger, unforgiveness, and bitterness to take root in our lives. We can overcome it all if we let go and let God!

Before we can "let God," or allow God to work in our lives, we have to "let go". One of my favorite Scriptures during the time I was going through the divorce was Psalm 55:22, which reads, "Cast your burden on the Lord, And He shall sustain you; He shall never permit the righteous to be moved".

First of all, we have to give it *ALL* to God, by letting go. Holding on to all that is hindering you, such as anger, resentment, bitterness, and unforgiveness is not the will of God. All of the things that we choose to hold on to blocks God's love in our heart and causes it to harden. By simply recognizing and acknowledging our true thoughts and emotions and learning how to give it completely over to God (rather than venting or burying them), then He will remove them from us "as far as the east is from the west" (Psalm 103:12) and fill us with His Love as He has promised.

I have experienced pain from a divorce. In the midst of the pain, I had a difficult time with being able to see or understand what was going on. Through many sleepless nights and woe is me days, I stood on the Word of God. I am not going to say it was easy, because it was not. No matter how many people tried to encourage and pray for me, I still wondered "Why Me"! I can say that I was holding on to a lot of resentment toward different people, which did not make the pain go away, but increased it. That is why it is very important to release it totally to God.

So how did I overcome the pain of divorce? By keeping my eyes focused on God!

> *Let us throw off everything that hinders and the sin that so easily entangles. And let us run with perseverance the race marked out for us, fixing our eyes on Jesus, the pioneer and perfecter of faith. (Hebrew 12:1-2, NIV)*

Keeping my focus on God was the key to overcoming all the pain that I was experiencing and being surrounded by prayer warriors who stood in the gap and prayed for me when it was difficult for me to pray for myself. One other thing I learned was no matter who I told my story to for sympathy or to make me feel better, it was not the answer. By doing so, I had not given it completely to God. Basically, I was still trying to control the situation myself, which didn't lessen the pain, but increased it. This action only causes the healing process to take longer. God never designed us to take on what He has promised to do.

I had to completely forgive those who I believed were involved, give it to God and let it go. Not until then did the healing begin.

As we know, forgiving someone is not easy. Matthew 6:14-15 says:

> *For if ye forgive men their trespasses, your heavenly Father will also forgive you, But if ye forgive not men their trespasses, neither will your Father forgive your trespasses.*

That Scripture speaks for itself. If we don't forgive others, how can we expect God to forgive us for the things we do. Think of it this way, we are all God's children. In John 15:12, Jesus commands us to love one another, as He has loved us. If we are bitter or hold unforgiveness against anyone, then we don't love them as Christ loves us.

By refusing to forgive, you are keeping yourself as the victim. Forgiving someone does NOT mean you are condoning what they did. It does not mean you approve of what they did. It means that you no longer hold yourself as the victim and you have released the hold they had on you. It also opens us up for God to forgive us and start the healing process in our lives. What a magnificent blessing forgiveness really is!!!

The next thing we must learn to do is embrace the pain of being divorced. Ouch!!! I know. That does not feel good.

We need to learn to stop running from the pain and face it head on. 1 Peter 2:19 says:

> *For it is commendable if a man bears up under the pain of unjust suffering because he is conscious of God.*

The word *charis* is the Greek word for grace. God gives grace during our suffering that he might bless us to endure and that we may find favor in His grace.

> *But he said to me, "My grace is sufficient for you, for my power is made perfect in weakness." Therefore I will boast all the more gladly about my weaknesses, so that Christ's power may rest on me. (2 Corinthians 12:9)*

Denying that you are divorced is the same as not accepting the truth that you are divorced. Accepting it will set you free to receive all that God has in store for you. Move Forward!

PAIN FROM LOSING A JOB

The pain of losing a job and becoming unemployed is unbearable. Having a job is part of our identity, so when it is taken from us, we may not know "who" we are anymore.

There is a feeling of failure, even if it's a layoff. You can do everything right and still get laid off.

When a person is laid-off from a job, they may become puzzled and confused, especially when they were an excellent employee, there were no complaints, and they received excellent evaluations, but still the day came when they were called into the boss' office to hear, "I am sorry, but we have to let you go." In most cases, it just does not make sense. At that point, their emotions can kick in, where they become upset and then begin to wonder how they are going to make it. During the process, some may fail to praise God for those doors being closed while having an expectation that He has something greater. Instead, the first thought is often, "I am an unemployment statistic."

The pain of losing a job can impact a person emotionally, physically and mentally. As I stated before, no matter what pain or problems we may face in life, we must continue to FOCUS on GOD!!!

God is true and faithful to His Word and He won't put more on us than we can bear. All we have to do is trust Him!!! He is "Jehovah-Jireh," which means God will provide.

> *But thou shalt remember the Lord thy God: for it is He that giveth thee power to get wealth. (Deuteronomy 8:18)*

During the times when I was unemployed, I can say that He supplied all my needs. Let's not get it twisted. Sometimes we may ask God for something and it may not be a need but a want. Note, the Scripture says "all your needs".

And my God will supply all your needs according to His riches in glory in Christ Jesus. (Philippians 4:19)

There was one particular time while I was unemployed that the rent was due and I did not know where I was going to get the money from. (Note: Even though I was collecting unemployment, it still wasn't enough to pay the rent and bills.) I started to get frustrated, panicked, and worried. The day before the rent was due, God provided; He made a way out of no way for my rent to be paid. He then said to me, "Why are you getting frustrated over something you have no control over. I got this!"

From that day on, I said I was not going to worry. The next month, I began speaking over my situation every morning when I woke up. Three days before the rent was due the following month, I saw God's hands in the midst of it. The first day, I checked my account and noticed there was unexpected money. I thought it was a glitch in the computer. I logged off and logged back on to see the same amount. I called the bank to find out if it was a mistake. They told me it was a bank transfer to my account but couldn't determine who put it there. All I could say was "Thank you Lord"!!! On the next day, I was blessed with four checks; one someone placed in my hands and the other three were received through the mail. Look how awesome our God is. But the blessings did not stop there. The very next morning on my way out, one of my special sisters in Christ was driving around the parking lot trying to remember where I lived. Once she spotted me, she called my name. I asked her why she was over in my area so early in the morning. She stated that she was being obedient and was told to be a blessing to me and put money in my hand.

When God says He will pour you out a blessing that there shall not be room enough to receive it, He truly means it. During those three days, He blessed me with enough to pay the rent for the upcoming month.

God wants us to depend on Him and trust His Word at all times, and not only when we are in desperate need of Him. As long as we are working and everything seems to be going smoothly, we tend to forget God. God wants us to trust and believe Him to His Word at all times.

Do not lose heart by focusing on your circumstances, but focus on The Provider.

> *But seek first the kingdom of God and his righteousness, and all these things will be added to you. (Matthew 6:33)*

Remember, millions of others have faced job loss and lived to tell about it. Many successful people have lost their jobs, only to go on to better things, even to have their own business and be successful. Losing a job is not a reflection of your worth as a person, or even on the quality of your work. With the right attitude, you can use the opportunity to do a little reflecting, exercise your faith and discover the plan and purpose God has for you to include considering new possibilities that may well prove to be more rewarding to you personally and financially.

PAIN FROM REJECTION

Rejection is very painful and hurts to the core of the heart. Rejection attacks your self-esteem and self-worth. Rejection affects your emotions and every area of your life. Being rejected will lead you to live in bondage, if you continue to hold on to it.

Some of the causes of rejection are past hurt, the death of a loved one, divorce, and even childhood experiences.

In our daily lives we are prone to trusting and being accepted by others, whether it's a spouse, family member or a close friend. During the time that we are establishing a relationship and once we have built a solid bond with that person, it most likely never crosses our mind that the relationship is going to end, but I am here to tell you that relationships do come and go. The only solid relationship we can count on is the one with Jesus Christ. He promises that He will never leave us nor forsake us.

So what do we do when we have been rejected? First of all, pray and ask the Lord to release you from all negative feelings associated with it. Forgive the person(s) who has hurt you. If possible, reach out to those who have harmed you and tell them that you forgive them for their actions.

> *"Moreover if your brother sins against you, go and tell him his fault between you and him alone. If he hears you, you have gained your brother. But if he will not hear, take with you one or two more, that 'by the mouth of two or three witnesses every word may be established." Matthew 18:15-16(NKJV)*

Last but not least, stop denying yourself. Accept and know who you really are in Christ.

When I was in 8th grade, I experienced rejection like never before. There was a girl who was my best friend (at least I thought she was). She lived down the street from me, but closer to the school. Every morning I would walk to her house and we would walk to school together. This went on for months. One morning, I went to her house and she said that she wasn't walking with me. I didn't understand why so I went alone. After school I noticed that she was with a group of girls who never did like me, and to this day, I still don't know why. As they were walking behind me, they began to burn my coat with a lighter, until two of my class mates stopped them.

That wasn't all. One day, after Physical Education class, I went to the locker room to change back into my clothes, only to find they were missing. I could see the girls standing over to the side laughing. One of them went in the bathroom stall and said out loud that someone's clothes were in the toilet. Yes, they were mine, and yes I was upset, but on the other hand, I was thanking God for Home Economics class. There they had a dryer where I was able to dry my clothes.

Because I didn't understand the rhyme or reason why they did what they did, I began to experience rejection from past hurts. It caused me to be a "people pleaser". I always thought that in order to have friends and be accepted by people that I had to do everything and anything that was required to please them. In the Kingdom of God, we all know that is a lie from the pit of hell. You do not need to compromise who you are in order to be accepted by others. Once I was healed and set free from rejection of past hurts, I was free from co-dependency on others. You have to know that you know that you know who you are in Christ!!!

I will praise thee; for I am fearfully and wonderfully made: marvellous are thy works; and that my soul knoweth right well. (Psalm 139:14)

God's desire is for you to know who you really are, and know how much He loves you, accepts you, and appreciates you, so that you can live out the fullness of what He has ordained you to be.

And to know the love of Christ, which passeth knowledge, that ye might be filled with all the fullness of God. (Ephesians 3:19)

Jesus was rejected and despised more than any of us. Through it all He endured, He overcame the persecution, and He forgave.

If you are in Christ, you will be rejected by people.

Remember the word that I said to you, 'A servant is not greater than his master.' If they persecuted me, they will also persecute you. (John 15:20, NKJV)

Know that you have the Victory over rejection when you choose to believe the Lord and find your acceptance in Him.

1 Corinthians 6:19-20 (NKJV) says:

Or do you not know that your body is the temple of the Holy Spirit who is in you, whom you have from God, and you are not your own? For you were bought at a price; therefore glorify God in your body and in your spirit, which are God's.

Receive that you belong to God, you are loved, you are accepted, and you are worthy!!!

REJOICE IN THE MIDST OF YOUR PAIN

By identifying the type of pain we are in and responding with the kind of faith that is appropriate to what is going on, we can discover the joy of the Lord in the midst of the pain. We must learn how to rejoice in our trials. This may be easier said than done. No one is happy when they are going through, but it does not mean it's the end. James 1:2-4 says:

> *My brethren, count it all joy when you fall into various trials, knowing that the testing of your faith produces patience. But let patience have its perfect work, that you may be perfect and complete, lacking nothing.*

No matter how we feel, we must know that God is always there for us. We must learn how to stay in peace through the storm and keep our joy. Know that God does not remove difficulties; He uses them for our good and for His glory.

Sometimes pain and suffering in the life of one person can result in advancement in the life of another person.

Although Paul was imprisoned when he wrote to the Philippians, his hardships didn't alarm him. His goal was to preach the gospel, and he did not question that goal just because he had been arrested. He made the most of the circumstances and proclaimed Christ to his captors. Paul stated that his imprisonment helped to advance the Gospel. (Philippians 1:12-14).

It's not easy to have a peace of mind when we are facing various trials. As a born again Christian, Christ resides in us, and since He has overcome the world, we can overcome all obstacles through Him. He is the Prince of Peace!

> *These things I have spoken to you, that in me you may have peace. In the world you will have tribulation; but be of good cheer, I have overcome the world." (John 16:33)*
>
> *Jesus is our Prince of peace. (Isaiah 9:6)*

In the next chapter we will see the purpose which is discovered through our pain. There is a purpose in your pain!!!!

Chapter 2. The Purpose

But indeed for this purpose I have raised you up, that I may show my power in you, and that my name may be declared in all the earth. (Exodus 9:16)

Regardless of what you have gone through or what may face next, always remember that your pain has purpose! Every test, every trial, and every hardship has pain associated with it, but I want to encourage you to respond differently each time. Learn from your last experience so you won't repeat it again.

Know that God didn't send all the craziness that is happening in your life, but He can and will use it for His glory. When it's all said and done, there is glory for your story, and our main purpose is to glorify God, which is done when we fulfill the purpose He has for us.

God has given each one of us a unique way to fulfilling His purpose for our lives. His purpose in allowing trials and tribulations in our lives is to develop us into His image and to make us stronger for the journey set before us. Also, it will change our conduct and refine our character, providing that we don't let bitterness, unbelief or discouragement rob us of the treasure.

In 2 Corinthians 4:8, God's Word says:

> *We are hard pressed on all sides but never crushed; perplexed, but not in despair; persecuted but never abandoned; struck down, but not destroyed.*

The storms of this life may rock your boat, but Jesus has promised that you will get to your final destination as long as you keep your eyes stayed on Him.

FINDING YOUR PURPOSE

Each one of us was born with a specific God given purpose. You are not an accident.

> *The Lord has made everything for its purpose, even the wicked for the day of trouble. (Proverbs 16:40, ESV)*

So you are probably wondering, "How can I find my specific purpose in life?" Start off by asking God to reveal it to you. Pray and ask Him to show you a vision. God wants you to discover the purpose He has for your life, and He will make it known to you. Even the pains, trials, or tribulations that you have gone through can very well be tied to your purpose.

After finding your purpose in life, begin using the gifts that God has placed inside of you to do whatever it is that you are supposed to be doing. Never allow fear, self, doubt, and what others may think steal your God ordained purpose.

People may ask if you are sure that is what God called you to do or they may suggest that you seek God a little longer to ensure you are hearing from Him, nevertheless you must go with what God has spoken to you. Once you are certain that what you are doing is from God, do not listen to the naysayers. It's a trick of the enemy to distract you from your destiny and cause you to doubt yourself.

Never allow hopelessness to stop you from discovering your purpose. God has a plan for you and this plan is outlined in His Word. Continue to pray daily and seek Him often concerning your purpose.

> *Rejoicing in hope; patient in tribulation; continuing instant in prayer. (Romans 12:12)*

Once you realize your purpose, you must take action. Taking action with God's power that flows through you is the next step.

> *For it is God who works in you to will and to act in order to fulfill his good purpose. (Philippians 2:13)*

When God gives you the vision and purpose for your life, He also gives you the power to fulfill it! Remember, your purpose is yours and cannot be accomplished by anyone else but you. Each of us must seek to fulfill our own purpose!

TAKING ACTION

Do not be afraid to rise up and take action in what God has laid upon your heart to do. God speaks to us in many ways. As you continue to seek God, He will reveal your purpose to you. It may be revealed through His Word, a vision, dream or even a person. However He reveals it, He will also show you the plan for how to fulfill it. When there is a plan on the inside of you that you cannot suppress and when it is in line with the Word of God, it will help you to know that it is from God.

Letting Go and Letting God!

When you are living a purposeful life, you die to yourself, and come to the conclusion that you cannot make things happen in your own strength, but through God all things are possible. You must also realize that because God loves us, He will never mislead or misguide us.

Through His power working in you, your purpose will be fulfilled. Once this happens, you will know because you will begin to feel whole, complete and at peace with whatever God has called you to do.

> *Acquaint now yourself with Him [agree with God and show yourself to be conformed to His will] and be at peace; by that [you shall prosper and great] good shall come to you. (Job 22:21, AMP)*

From the pain I experienced through being tortured by females in elementary school, going through a devastating divorce and being unemployed, that is when I discovered my purpose.

During my quiet time with God, He spoke the words Pure N' Heart to me. I wasn't quite sure where He was leading me by speaking those words to me. One day while speaking to a close friend, I shared with her how God had spoken those words to me and how it was so strong in my spirit. As I stated earlier, God can reveal things through a person. She said, "Pure N Heart is your ministry." As I prayed and asked God for clarity, He did just that.

Pure N' Heart Ministries was birthed in September 2009. Through all my brokenness, God is now using me to minister healing and deliverance to the broken hearted. Glory be to God!!!

God will use those who are willing to minister not out of their strengths, but out of their weaknesses. Sometimes He will use your own personal tragedy as a testimony for you to minister to people who are going through the exact thing or similar to what you have experienced.

The story of Apostle Paul is a good example of how he pursued his destiny. The moment Paul embraced his destiny and began to fulfill his purpose, he began an adventure that lasted for the rest of his life. He had no idea where his new purpose was going to take him, but he lived it fearlessly. He saw many miracles. He raised the dead and healed the sick. He witnessed to kings. He brought blessing and comfort to thousands of believers - most of whom he, himself, led to Christ. Of course, he also ended up in jail a few times.

The point to all of this is when you embrace your purpose, you will embark on an adventure that will last for the rest of your life. You will see and do things that you never would have imagined doing, even though you are seeing it with your own eyes. You will be used to accomplish great things for God, and you will see firsthand the value you have because you yielded to your purpose.

> *Many plans are in a man's mind, but it is the Lord's purpose for him that will stand. (Proverbs 19: 21)*

Keep your eyes on the Lord and you will not lose sight of your life's purpose. His purpose and destiny will last throughout eternity and know that He will always equip you to carry out His will.

I do not believe He calls us without equipping us. When God gives us a vision for something, we often wonder how it can be accomplished when we do not have what is necessary to get started, but when you step out on faith, God will provide your every need. He is always working in us, making us what we ought to be in order to 'accomplish' that which is pleasing in His sight.

Be persistent to push past your pain and proceed with the process to pray, plan, and pursue the calling in which God has gifted you!!!

Chapter 3. The Promise

> *For all the promises of God in Him are Yes, and in Him Amen, to the glory of God through us. (2 Corinthians 1:20)*

Have you ever had someone make a promise to you and not keep it? A promise is an undertaking from one person to another, guaranteeing to do or give something in the future. Unlike men who make promises and speak of their intentions, but then often fail to keep them, God's promises are in His Word, and cannot be broken.

> *God is not man, that he should lie, or a son of man, that he should change his mind. Has he said, and will he not do it? Or has he spoken, and will he not fulfill it? (Numbers 23:19, ESV)*

The promises of God are concerned with the future, both of mankind and of the world. In order for the promise to become effective for any individual, we must believe and ask for them in faith.

> *You do not have, because you do not ask. (James 4:2, ESV)*

God's promises deal with all aspects of life including our health, relationships, finances, family, work, love, etc. We have to search God's Word, find His promises, speak His promises over our lives, hold onto them, and lastly thank Him for His promises that will be fulfilled in our lives.

Whenever we speak God's promises over our lives, its manifestation draws near to us. Whenever you thank Him for them, you remain in His will. So for example, the devil tries to tell you something like "You are sick and you will never be well", you say, "No I don't think so, God promised me that...by His stripes I am healed." Then you turn your attention to God and say "God I thank you for your promise…it's in you that I put my trust." Even at times when it seems the hardest, do not give up. Refuse to entertain satan's thoughts because he is not worth your time! His plan is to steal, kill and destroy God's purpose for your life.

> *The thief cometh not, but for to steal, and to kill, and to destroy: I am come that they might have life, and that they might have it more abundantly. (John 10:10)*

If you ever come to a place in life where you feel like you have absolutely nothing but a promise from God, then you have enough. Always strive to focus on God's promises and not your problems.

PERSEVERE UNTIL YOU SEE THE PROMISE

> *You need to persevere so that when you have done the will of God, you will receive what He has promised. (Hebrews 10:36)*

What do you believe God for today? Promotion? Healing? Stronger relationships? Deliverance? God has promised all these things to you in His Word because it is His heart for you to live in blessing and wholeness.

When you follow the will of God by obeying His Word and precepts, it opens the door for His promises to be fulfilled in your life. Don't give up! Perseverance will carry you to the promise.

Perseverance means that you are focused, and that you believe what God says about your situation. It is looking away from distractions and any negative, defeating thoughts.

I recently had to travel to St. Louis and during my flight, God gave me revelation about staying focused. While looking out the window, I noticed how thick the clouds were and it was hard to see through them. As the plane continued to reach its altitude, it began to shake, and there was a lot of turbulence, but as it proceeded to climb higher and higher, the shaking began to stop and the sky was very clear. Then the Holy Spirit spoke to me and said, "This is how it is when my people are facing trials and tribulations. Many cannot see beyond their problems because they are focusing on their problems. All they see is a cloudy vision, but if they will focus on me, then they will see the clearer picture instead of a cloudy vision."

Perseverance looks away from discouragement and looks to the Word of God. Perseverance has a voice, and it says things like, "No weapon formed against me shall prosper! If God is for me, who can be against me! I am more than a conqueror through Christ Jesus!"

Whatever you believe for today, keep believing! Stand strong and fight the good fight of faith. Ask God to give you endurance, perseverance and patience so that you can see His promises fulfilled in every area of your life!

HAVING ALL THAT YOU NEED

But my God shall supply all your need according to his riches in glory by Christ Jesus. (Philippians 4:19)

We serve a God of abundance! He is more than enough! No matter what is on your "plate" of life, God wants to pour out His abundant grace upon you. One of the meanings of grace is God's good will, loving kindness and favor. His grace keeps us, strengthens us and causes us to increase. In fact, He's already extending that grace to you right now; all you have to do is open your heart and humbly receive it by faith.

Humility is an important key to receiving God's grace. If we are seeking our own way, it blocks Him from working in our lives, but when we are humble, then He will empower us by His grace. Notice in 2 Corinthians 9:8 where it states that by His grace you will have everything you need at all times...that's living in abundance! And when you are living in abundance, you are equipped to be a blessing to those around you. Today, seek His ways first and allow Him to empower you by His grace.

FILLED TO OVERFLOWING

Honor the LORD with your wealth, with the first fruits of all your crops; then your barns will be filled to overflowing, and your vats will brim over with new wine. (Proverbs 3:9–10)

God wants you to be blessed and successful in this life. He desires to multiply and increase you so that you can be a blessing to other people. He wants to fill you to overflowing. In other words, He wants you to have so much that you can't help but bless the people around you!

God's very nature is giving. All throughout Scripture, we see that giving is a demonstration of His love. When you are a giver, you are displaying who He is and reflecting His character. Notice that when you give to God first, it opens the door to God's overflowing blessing. He promises to increase you so much that you can't even contain it. You will be in a position to bless others and communicate His love everywhere you go.

Whatsoever you are going through today, remember God has fulfilled all His promises to you through the finished work of Christ Jesus. Get ready to be filled to overflowing!

GOD SAID IT, I BELIEVE IT, THAT SETTLES IT!

Appendix: List of God's Promises

Exod 34:5-7 5And the LORD descended in the cloud, and stood with him there, and proclaimed the name of the LORD. 6And the LORD passed by before him, and proclaimed, The LORD, The LORD God, merciful and gracious, longsuffering, and abundant in goodness and truth, 7Keeping mercy for thousands, forgiving iniquity and transgression and sin, and that will by no means clear [the guilty]; visiting the iniquity of the fathers upon the children, and upon the children's children, unto the third and to the fourth [generation].

Lev 26:8 And five of you shall chase an hundred, and an hundred of you shall put ten thousand to flight: and your enemies shall fall before you by the sword.

Num 6:22-27 22And the LORD spake unto Moses, saying, 23 Speak unto Aaron and unto his sons, saying, On this wise ye shall bless the children of Israel, saying unto them, 24The LORD bless thee, and keep thee: 25The LORD make his face shine upon thee, and be gracious unto thee: 26 The LORD lift up his countenance upon thee, and give thee peace. 27And they shall put my name upon the children of Israel; and I will bless them.

Deut 4:29 But if from thence thou shalt seek the LORD thy God, thou shalt find [him], if thou seek him with all thy heart and with all thy soul.

Deut 11:25 There shall no man be able to stand before you: [for] the LORD your God shall lay the fear of you and the dread of you upon all the land that ye shall tread upon, as he hath said unto you.

Deut 23:5 Nevertheless the LORD thy God would not hearken unto Balaam; but the LORD thy God turned the curse into a blessing unto thee, because the LORD thy God loved thee.

Deut 28:7 The LORD shall cause thine enemies that rise up against thee to be smitten before thy face: they shall come out against thee one way, and flee before thee seven ways.

Deut 32:10 He found him in a desert land, and in the waste howling wilderness; he led him about, he instructed him, he kept him as the apple of his eye.

Job 16:20 My friends scorn me: [but] mine eye poureth out [tears] unto God.

Ps 12:6 The words of the LORD [are] pure words: [as] silver tried in a furnace of earth, purified seven times.

Ps 17:8 Keep me as the apple of the eye, hide me under the shadow of thy wings,

Ps 29:4 The voice of the LORD [is] powerful; the voice of the LORD [is] full of majesty.

Ps 34:8 O taste and see that the LORD [is] good: blessed [is] the man [that] trusteth in him.

Ps 34:18 The LORD [is] nigh unto them that are of a broken heart; and saveth such as be of a contrite spirit.

Ps 45:1 To the chief Musician upon Shoshannim, for the sons of Korah, Maschil, A Song of loves. My heart is inditing a good matter: I speak of the things which I have made touching the king: my tongue [is] the pen of a ready writer.

Ps 50:15 And call upon me in the day of trouble: I will deliver thee, and thou shalt glorify me.

Ps 56:8 Thou tellest my wanderings: put thou my tears into thy bottle: [are they] not in thy book?

Ps 61:2 From the end of the earth will I cry unto thee, when my heart is overwhelmed: lead me to the rock [that] is higher than I.

Ps 84:11 For the LORD God [is] a sun and shield: the LORD will give grace and glory: no good [thing] will he withhold from them that walk uprightly.

Ps 91:1 He that dwelleth in the secret place of the most High shall abide under the shadow of the Almighty.

Ps 103:3-5 [3]Who forgiveth all thine iniquities; who healeth all thy diseases; [4]Who redeemeth thy life from destruction; who crowneth thee with loving kindness and tender mercies; [5]Who satisfieth thy mouth with good [things; so that] thy youth is renewed like the eagle's.

Ps 103:8 The LORD [is] merciful and gracious, slow to anger, and plenteous in mercy

Ps 103:12-13 [12]As far as the east is from the west, [so] far hath he removed our transgressions from us. [13]Like as a father pitieth [his] children, [so] the LORD pitieth them that fear him.

Ps 109:5 And they have rewarded me evil for good, and hatred for my love.

Ps 111:10 The fear of the LORD [is] the beginning of wisdom: a good understanding have all they that do [his commandments]: his praise endureth for ever.

Ps 119:105 NUN. Thy word [is] a lamp unto my feet, and a light unto my path.

Ps 126:5 They that sow in tears shall reap in joy.

Ps 127:2 [It is] vain for you to rise up early, to sit up late, to eat the bread of sorrows: [for] so he giveth his beloved sleep.

Prov 5:18-20 18Let thy fountain be blessed: and rejoice with the wife of thy youth. 19[Let her be as] the loving hind and pleasant roe; let her breasts satisfy thee at all times; and be thou ravished always with her love. 20And why wilt thou, my son, be ravished with a strange woman, and embrace the bosom of a stranger?

Prov 6:30-31 30[Men] do not despise a thief, if he steal to satisfy his soul when he is hungry; 31But [if] he be found, he shall restore sevenfold; he shall give all the substance of his house.

Prov 9:10 The fear of the LORD [is] the beginning of wisdom: and the knowledge of the holy [is] understanding.

Prov 10:22 The blessing of the LORD, it maketh rich, and he addeth no sorrow with it.

Prov 17:9 He that covereth a transgression seeketh love; but he that repeateth a matter separateth [very] friends.

Prov 18:21 Death and life [are] in the power of the tongue: and they that love it shall eat the fruit thereof.

Prov 19:17 He that hath pity upon the poor lendeth unto the LORD; and that which he hath given will he pay him again.

Prov 26:18-19 18As a mad [man] who casteth firebrands, arrows, and death, 19So [is] the man [that] deceiveth his neighbour, and saith, Am not I in sport?

Prov 26:25 When he speaketh fair, believe him not: for [there are] seven abominations in his heart.

Eccl 12:12 And further, by these, my son, be admonished: of making many books [there is] no end; and much study [is] a weariness of the flesh.

Song 8:6-7 6 Set me as a seal upon thine heart, as a seal upon thine arm: for love [is] strong as death; jealousy [is] cruel as the grave: the coals thereof [are] coals of fire, [which hath a] most vehement flame. 7Many waters cannot quench love, neither can the floods drown it: if [a] man would give all the substance of his house for love, it would utterly be contemned.

Isa 25:4 For thou hast been a strength to the poor, a strength to the needy in his distress, a refuge from the storm, a shadow from the heat, when the blast of the terrible ones [is] as a storm [against] the wall.

Isa 25:8 He will swallow up death in victory; and the Lord GOD will wipe away tears from off all faces; and the rebuke of his people shall he take away from off all the earth: for the LORD hath spoken [it].

Isa 41:10 Fear thou not; for I [am] with thee: be not dismayed; for I [am] thy God: I will strengthen thee; yea, I will help thee; yea, I will uphold thee with the right hand of my righteousness.

Isa 43:4 Since thou wast precious in my sight, thou hast been honourable, and I have loved thee: therefore will I give men for thee, and people for thy life.

Isa 45:2-3 [2]I will go before thee, and make the crooked places straight: I will break in pieces the gates of brass, and cut in sunder the bars of iron: [3]And I will give thee the treasures of darkness, and hidden riches of secret places, that thou mayest know that I, the LORD, which call [thee] by thy name, [am] the God of Israel.

Isa 48:17 Thus saith the LORD, thy Redeemer, the Holy One of Israel; I [am] the LORD thy God which teacheth thee to profit, which leadeth thee by the way [that] thou shouldest go.

Isa 49:15-16 [15]Can a woman forget her sucking child, that she should not have compassion on the son of her womb? yea, they may forget, yet will I not forget thee. [16]Behold, I have graven thee upon the palms of [my] hands; thy walls [are] continually before me.

Isa 51:3 For the LORD shall comfort Zion: he will comfort all her waste places; and he will make her wilderness like Eden, and her desert like the garden of the LORD; joy and gladness shall be found therein, thanksgiving, and the voice of melody.

Isa 54:10 For the mountains shall depart, and the hills be removed; but my kindness shall not depart from thee, neither shall the covenant of my peace be removed, saith the LORD that hath mercy on thee.

Isa 54:15 Behold, they shall surely gather together, [but] not by me: whosoever shall gather together against thee shall fall for thy sake.

Isa 54:17 No weapon that is formed against thee shall prosper; and every tongue [that] shall rise against thee in judgment thou shalt condemn. This [is] the heritage of the servants of the LORD, and their righteousness [is] of me, saith the LORD.

Isa 55:11 So shall my word be that goeth forth out of my mouth: it shall not return unto me void, but it shall accomplish that which I please, and it shall prosper [in the thing] whereto I sent it.

Isa 57:18-19 [18]I have seen his ways, and will heal him: I will lead him also, and restore comforts unto him and to his mourners. [19]I create the fruit of the lips; Peace, peace to [him that is] far off, and to [him that is] near, saith the LORD; and I will heal him.

Isa 59:1 Behold, the LORD'S hand is not shortened, that it cannot save; neither his ear heavy, that it cannot hear:

Isa 60:19 The sun shall be no more thy light by day; neither for brightness shall the moon give light unto thee: but the LORD shall be unto thee an everlasting light, and thy God thy glory.

Isa 61:1 The Spirit of the Lord GOD [is] upon me; because the LORD hath anointed me to preach good tidings unto the meek; he hath sent me to bind up the brokenhearted, to proclaim liberty to the captives, and the opening of the prison to [them that are] bound;

Jer 1:5 Before I formed thee in the belly I knew thee; and before thou camest forth out of the womb I sanctified thee, [and] I ordained thee a prophet unto the nations. KJV

Jer 1:9 Then the LORD put forth his hand, and touched my mouth. And the LORD said unto me, Behold, I have put my words in thy mouth.

Jer 1:12 Then said the LORD unto me, Thou hast well seen: for I will hasten my word to perform it.

Jer 1:19 And they shall fight against thee; but they shall not prevail against thee; for I [am] with thee, saith the LORD, to deliver thee.

Jer 3:15 And I will give you pastors according to mine heart, which shall feed you with knowledge and understanding.

Jer 15:19 Therefore thus saith the LORD, If thou return, then will I bring thee again, [and] thou shalt stand before me: and if thou take forth the precious from the vile, thou shalt be as my mouth: let them return unto thee; but return not thou unto them.

Jer 20:11 But the LORD [is] with me as a mighty terrible one: therefore my persecutors shall stumble, and they shall not prevail: they shall be greatly ashamed; for they shall not prosper: [their] everlasting confusion shall never be forgotten.

Jer 23:29 [Is] not my word like as a fire? saith the LORD; and like a hammer [that] breaketh the rock in pieces?

Jer 29:11 For I know the thoughts that I think toward you, saith the LORD, thoughts of peace, and not of evil, to give you an expected end.

Jer 31:3 The LORD hath appeared of old unto me, [saying], Yea, I have loved thee with an everlasting love: therefore with lovingkindness have I drawn thee.

Jer 33:3 Call unto me, and I will answer thee, and shew thee great and mighty things, which thou knowest not.

Hos 6:6 For I desired mercy, and not sacrifice; and the knowledge of God more than burnt offerings.

Hos 11:4 I drew them with cords of a man, with bands of love: and I was to them as they that take off the yoke on their jaws, and I laid meat unto them.

Hos 12:6 Therefore turn thou to thy God: keep mercy and judgment, and wait on thy God continually.

Joel 2:13 And rend your heart, and not your garments, and turn unto the LORD your God: for he [is] gracious and merciful, slow to anger, and of great kindness, and repenteth him of the evil.

Mic 6:8 He hath shewed thee, O man, what [is] good; and what doth the LORD require of thee, but to do justly, and to love mercy, and to walk humbly with thy God?

Zeph 3:17 The LORD thy God in the midst of thee [is] mighty; he will save, he will rejoice over thee with joy; he will rest in his love, he will joy over thee with singing.

Zech 2:8 For thus saith the LORD of hosts; After the glory hath he sent me unto the nations which spoiled you: for he that toucheth you toucheth the apple of his eye.

Zech 4:6 Then he answered and spake unto me, saying, This [is] the word of the LORD unto Zerubbabel, saying, Not by might, nor by power, but by my spirit, saith the LORD of hosts.

Matt 5:3-12 [3]Blessed [are] the poor in spirit: for theirs is the kingdom of heaven. [4]Blessed [are] they that mourn: for they shall be comforted. [5]Blessed [are] the meek: for they shall inherit the earth. [6]Blessed [are] they which do hunger and thirst after righteousness: for they shall be filled. [7]Blessed [are] the merciful: for they shall obtain mercy. [8]Blessed [are] the pure in heart: for they shall see God. [9]Blessed [are] the peacemakers: for they shall be called the children of God. [10] Blessed [are] they which are persecuted for righteousness' sake: for theirs is the kingdom of heaven. [11]Blessed are ye, when [men] shall revile you, and persecute [you], and shall say all manner of evil against you falsely, for my sake. [12] Rejoice, and be exceeding glad: for great [is] your reward in heaven: for so persecuted they the prophets which were before you.

Matt 6:33 But seek ye first the kingdom of God, and his righteousness; and all these things shall be added unto you.

Matt 17:20 And Jesus said unto them, Because of your unbelief: for verily I say unto you, If ye have faith as a grain of mustard seed, ye shall say unto this mountain, Remove hence to yonder place; and it shall remove; and nothing shall be impossible unto you.

Matt 18:20 For where two or three are gathered together in my name, there am I in the midst of them.

Matt 21:22 And all things, whatsoever ye shall ask in prayer, believing, ye shall receive.

Mark 1:15 And saying, The time is fulfilled, and the kingdom of God is at hand: repent ye, and believe the gospel.

Mark 9:23 Jesus said unto him, If thou canst believe, all things [are] possible to him that believeth.

Mark 11:23 For verily I say unto you, That whosoever shall say unto this mountain, Be thou removed, and be thou cast into the sea; and shall not doubt in his heart, but shall believe that those things which he saith shall come to pass; he shall have whatsoever he saith.

Luke 7:47 Wherefore I say unto thee, Her sins, which are many, are forgiven; for she loved much: but to whom little is forgiven, [the same] loveth little.

Luke 10:19 Behold, I give unto you power to tread on serpents and scorpions, and over all the power of the enemy: and nothing shall by any means hurt you.

Luke 17:6 And the Lord said, If ye had faith as a grain of mustard seed, ye might say unto this sycamine tree, Be thou plucked up by the root, and be thou planted in the sea; and it should obey you

John 1:1-5 1In the beginning was the Word, and the Word
was with God, and the Word was God. 2The same was in the
beginning with God. 3All things were made by him; and

without him was not any thing made that was made. [4]In him was life; and the life was the light of men. [5]And the light shineth in darkness; and the darkness comprehended it not.

John 1:12 But as many as received him, to them gave he power to become the sons of God, [even] to them that believe on his name:

John 6:63 It is the spirit that quickeneth; the flesh profiteth nothing: the words that I speak unto you, [they] are spirit, and [they] are life.

John 10:10 The thief cometh not, but for to steal, and to kill, and to destroy: I am come that they might have life, and that they might have [it] more abundantly.

John 13:35 By this shall all [men] know that ye are my disciples, if ye have love one to another.

John 15:10 If ye keep my commandments, ye shall abide in my love; even as I have kept my Father's commandments, and abide in his love.

John 15:13 Greater love hath no man than this, that a man lay down his life for his friends.

John 17:3 And this is life eternal, that they might know thee the only true God, and Jesus Christ, whom thou hast sent.

John 17:26 And I have declared unto them thy name, and will declare [it]: that the love wherewith thou hast loved me may be in them, and I in them.

Rom 5:8 But God commendeth his love toward us, in that, while we were yet sinners, Christ died for us. Rom 8:1

[There is] therefore now no condemnation to them which are in Christ Jesus, who walk not after the flesh, but after the Spirit.

Rom 8:5 For they that are after the flesh do mind the things of the flesh; but they that are after the Spirit the things of the Spirit.

Rom 8:14 For as many as are led by the Spirit of God, they are the sons of God.

Rom 8:15 For ye have not received the spirit of bondage again to fear; but ye have received the Spirit of adoption, whereby we cry, Abba, Father.

Rom 8:26-27 [26]Likewise the Spirit also helpeth our infirmities: for we know not what we should pray for as we ought: but the Spirit itself maketh intercession for us with groanings which cannot be uttered. [27]And he that searcheth the hearts knoweth what [is] the mind of the Spirit, because he maketh intercession for the saints according to [the will of] God.

Rom 8:28 And we know that all things work together for good to them that love God, to them who are the called according to [his] purpose

Rom 8:31 What shall we then say to these things? If God [be] for us, who [can be] against us?

Rom 8:37 Nay, in all these things we are more than conquerors through him that loved us.

Rom 10:10 For with the heart man believeth unto righteousness; and with the mouth confession is made unto salvation.

Rom 10:17 So then faith [cometh] by hearing, and hearing by the word of God.

Rom 12:20-21 [20]Therefore if thine enemy hunger, feed him; if he thirst, give him drink: for in so doing thou shalt heap coals of fire on his head. [21]Be not overcome of evil, but overcome evil with good.

Rom 13:8 Owe no man any thing, but to love one another: for he that loveth another hath fulfilled the law.

Rom 13:10 Love worketh no ill to his neighbour: therefore love [is] the fulfilling of the law.

1Cor 13:13 And now abideth faith, hope, charity, these three; but the greatest of these [is] charity.

1Cor 14:33 For God is not [the author] of confusion, but of peace, as in all churches of the saints.

2Cor 10:3-6 [3]For though we walk in the flesh, we do not war after the flesh: [4](For the weapons of our warfare [are] not carnal, but mighty through God to the pulling down of strong holds;) [5]Casting down imaginations, and every high thing that exalteth itself against the knowledge of God, and bringing into captivity every thought to the obedience of Christ; [6]And having in a readiness to revenge all disobedience, when your obedience is fulfilled.

Gal 5:22 But the fruit of the Spirit is love, joy, peace, longsuffering, gentleness, goodness, faith,

Gal 6:2 Bear ye one another's burdens, and so fulfill the law of Christ.

Eph 2:8 For by grace are ye saved through faith; and that not of yourselves: [it is] the gift of God:

Phil 4:8 Finally, brethren, whatsoever things are true, whatsoever things [are] honest, whatsoever things [are] just, whatsoever things [are] pure, whatsoever things [are] lovely, whatsoever things [are] of good report; if [there be] any virtue, and if [there be] any praise, think on these things.

1Tim 6:10 For the love of money is the root of all evil: which while some coveted after, they have erred from the faith, and pierced themselves through with many sorrows.

2Tim 1:7 For God hath not given us the spirit of fear; but of power, and of love, and of a sound mind.

Heb 4:12 For the word of God [is] quick, and powerful, and sharper than any two-edged sword, piercing even to the dividing asunder of soul and spirit, and of the joints and marrow, and [is] a discerner of the thoughts and intents of the heart.

Heb 11:1 Now faith is the substance of things hoped for, the evidence of things not seen.

Jas 4:7 Submit yourselves therefore to God. Resist the devil, and he will flee from you.

1Pet 5:7 Casting all your care upon him; for he careth for you.

1Pet 5:8 Be sober, be vigilant; because your adversary the devil, as a roaring lion, walketh about, seeking whom he may devour:

1John 4:4 Ye are of God, little children, and have overcome them: because greater is he that is in you, than he that is in the world.

1John 5:4 For whatsoever is born of God overcometh the world: and this is the victory that overcometh the world, [even] our faith.

1John 5:5 Who is he that overcometh the world, but he that believeth that Jesus is the Son of God?

Rev 7:17 For the Lamb which is in the midst of the throne shall feed them, and shall lead them unto living fountains of waters: and God shall wipe away all tears from their eyes.

Rev 12:11 And they overcame him by the blood of the Lamb, and by the word of their testimony; and they loved not their lives unto the death.

Rev 19:11-13 [11]And I saw heaven opened, and behold a white horse; and he that sat upon him [was] called Faithful and True, and in righteousness he doth judge and make war.
[12]His eyes [were] as a flame of fire, and on his head [were] many crowns; and he had a name written, that no man knew, but he himself. [13]And he [was] clothed with a vesture dipped in blood: and his name is called The Word of God.

Rev 21:4 And God shall wipe away all tears from their eyes; and there shall be no more death, neither sorrow, nor crying, neither shall there be any more pain: for the former things are passed away.

Rev 21:23 And the city had no need of the sun, neither of the moon, to shine in it: for the glory of God did lighten it, and the Lamb [is] the light thereof.

About the Author

Sandra Moore is a spirit-filled Woman of God, seeker of God's Kingdom and righteousness, and a pursuer of God's presence. She was born and raised in Buffalo, New York to Walter and Sarah Hill. Sandra was saved in 1973 and attended Friendship Baptist Church. In June 1985, she joined the United States Army. During her tour she served at Fort Devens, Massachusetts and the Republic of Panama.

Sandra has attended and completed the following classes: The Life University-School of The Prophets, Hermeneutics, E.V. Reeves School of Advanced Leadership, Beacon Institute - School of Theology at New Life Anointed Ministries Int'l.; School of the Prophets under Jimmie Reed Ministries and Christian International Ministries - Ministering Spiritual Gifts, and School of the Prophets under

Bishop Joseph A. McCargo, Kingdom Institute of Apostolic and Prophetic Studies. She is currently attending the Covenant Life Church in Alexandria, Virginia.

Sandra is the founder of Pure N' Heart Ministries, Inc., established on September 5, 2009, and President of Kingdom Builder Designs, LLC.

She truly loves God and has a heart to serve and lead God's people into a higher calling through Christ Jesus. Within this call of ministry, God has given her a vision to host annual Women's Conferences to bring healing and deliverance to their lives.

Sandra is the proud mother of four beautiful children - Carolyn, Tony, Nigel and Lionel. Sandra has a passion for giving and ministering the power of Jesus Christ into the lives of people she encounters. Her favorite scripture is Matthew 6:33: *Seek Ye First the Kingdom of God and His Righteousness, and all these things shall be added unto you as well.*

About Kingdom Journey Press

Kingdom Journey Press, Inc. is a full-service publishing company specializing in providing customized services to support our clients from the conception of an idea to getting HIStory to the masses! Since the time of inception and in conjunction with our umbrella organization, Kingdom Journey Enterprises, we have become recognized globally for our ability to establish a unique presence, while building relationships with partners and clients consisting of current and aspiring writers, and ministry, business, and community organizations.

Our services include:

- Manuscript Evaluation
- Coaching for current and aspiring authors
- Editing
- Cover and Print Layout Design
- Print and E-Book Format
- Copyright and Distribution
- Marketing and Sales Support

To contact us and to learn more information about our services, we invite you to visit our website at www.kjpressinc.com.

www.ingramcontent.com/pod-product-compliance
Lightning Source LLC
LaVergne TN
LVHW041235080426
835508LV00011B/1225
9780982700181